Jazz Has Frizz!

By Sascha Goddard

Jazz had a lot of frizz and fuzz.

She did not like it.

"I will get my fuzz cut off,"
said Jazz.
"It's a mess."

Jazz went to Dell.

"Dell, can you cut off all my fuzz?" said Jazz.

"I can," said Dell.

"But fuzz is fun! Frizz is tops! You will see."

"Yes, I will see, Dell," said Jazz.

Dell cuts.

Buzz, buzz, buzz!

Dell dips.

Dab, dab, dab!

"Hop up and see, Jazz!"
said Dell.

Jazz had a look.

She still had frizz,

but it was not a mess.

It was ... fun fuzz!

"Well?" said Dell.

"My frizz and fuzz are tops!"
said Jazz.

CHECKING FOR MEANING

1. Why did Jazz want her fuzz cut off? *(Literal)*

2. What did Dell do to make Jazz look better? *(Literal)*

3. If Dell was a person, what job would she have? *(Inferential)*

EXTENDING VOCABULARY

frizz	What does *frizz* mean in this story? What are some words we use to describe hair? E.g. curly, straight, long, short.
fuzz	What is *fuzz*? How is *fuzz* different to *frizz*?
still	What are two meanings of the word *still*? Use the word in sentences to show it has different meanings.

MOVING BEYOND THE TEXT

1. Why do people like having their hair styled?

2. Who cuts or trims your hair? Where do you go to have this done?

3. What are other things we can do to make ourselves feel better?

4. What does a hairdresser use to cut and style hair?

SPEED SOUNDS

| ff | ll | ss | zz |

PRACTICE WORDS

Jazz

frizz

fuzz

will

off

mess

Buzz

Frizz

Dell

still

Well

buzz